CW00422319

THE WORLD
ACCORDING TO
JULIUS
MALEMA

Written and compiled by

MAX DU PREEZ and **MANDY ROSSOUW**

KWELA BOOKS

Generous use has been made of the following websites
in order to verify the accuracy of Malema's statements:
www.citizen.co.za; www.cosatu.org.za; www.dispatch.co.za;
www.iafrica.com; www.iol.co.za; www.mg.co.za; www.news24.com;
www.politicsweb.co.za; www.polity.org.za; www.sowetan.co.za;
www.theherald.co.za; www.thetimes.co.za.

Kwela Books,
an imprint of NB Publishers,
40 Heerengracht, Cape Town, South Africa
PO Box 6525, Roggebaai, 8012, South Africa
www.kwela.com

Copyright © 2009 Kwela Books

All rights reserved
No part of this book may be reproduced or transmitted in any
form or by any electronic or mechanical means, including
photocopying and recording, or by any other information storage or
retrieval system, without written permission from the publisher

Cover image by Muntu Vilakazi
(courtesy of the photographer and *Sunday Times*)
Cover design by Hanneke du Toit
Typography by Nazli Jacobs
Set in Palatino
Printed and bound by Paarl Print,
Oosterland Street, Paarl, South Africa

First edition, first impression 2009

ISBN: 978-0-7957-0292-1

Foreword

In April 2007 few South Africans knew of the existence of a young man called Julius Sello Malema. But by the time the country held general elections in April 2009, his name and face had become as instantly recognisable as that of the new president himself.

By mid-2009 Malema, still only 28 years old, was one of the most blogged-about people in Africa. A Google search listed more than 100 000 English pages. Hardly a day goes by without some newspaper mentioning his name somewhere. He has even featured in a fast-food chain's advertising campaign, albeit as a puppet.

No previous president of the African National Congress Youth League, not even the controversial Peter Mokaba or the hot-headed Fikile Mbalula, Malema's immediate predecessor, has generated such strong emotion. Few public personalities have been subjected to as many jokes and as much abuse.

But it is also true that no Youth League president before him could claim to have played such a major role in an ANC election campaign as Malema did in 2009.

It would be generally true to say that Malema is despised and ridiculed by most white South Africans as well as people from other minority groups, even by sections of the urban black elite. His behaviour has often been cited as a reason for members of the black middle class abandoning the ANC and joining the breakaway Congress of the People (Cope).

Yet it is also true that among the black youth Malema has become a much-admired hero and his arrogant, crude defiance a representation of their fears, resentments and aspirations.

Mention Malema's name in any kind of company and you're bound to start debates around questions such as: is he simply a buffoon, or is he actually very smart? Is he an unguided missile, or is he doing some puppet master's bidding? Is the Zuma leadership unhappy with his statements, or do Malema's often outrageous utterances actually suit them? And: did Malema hurt or help the ANC during their 2009 election campaign?

Another question: is Julius Malema just an interesting individual, or does he represent something bigger in South African society? If he is a symbol, of what?

There are few answers in his office, in the ANC's headquarters at Luthuli House, Johannesburg. The large desk is shiny and empty. No papers or books or even a computer in sight, although he has said the Youth League supplied him with a laptop. A fancy living room suite with a glass coffee table adorns one corner, but there are no personal memorabilia like photographs to make the office his home away from home. From behind his desk he can look out onto the road where ministers and other dignitaries visiting Luthuli House park their cars. When his cellphone rings, the sound of a revolutionary song fills the room.

Malema's name was catapulted into the headlines with his shocking public declaration in June 2008: "Let us make it clear now: We are prepared to die for Zuma. Not only that, we are prepared to take up arms and kill for Zuma."

But his political career had started much earlier than that.

"

The early years

Malema was born on 3 March 1981 into a poverty-stricken township called Masakeng Zone 1 in Seshego, Limpopo. His father was absent; he was brought up by his mother, Flora, a domestic worker, and his grandmother, Sarah.

"You will find the poorest people in Masakeng," Malema says, "and my family was the poorest of the poor." He likes to refer to his "peasant" background in interviews. He told the *Sowetan* daily newspaper in April 2009: "Having gone to school without shoes or proper uniform and during lunch times not knowing where you will get your next meal, those are the conditions we grew up under."

Flora Malema was a devout Christian and not very politically inclined. When the young Julius ran into trouble at school, it was Granny Sarah who rushed to his defence – "my mother was afraid of the authorities". Julius soon grew much closer to his grandmother, who was, and still is, according to him, a committed ANC activist. In a rare glimpse into his private life, he told Talk Radio 702's Jenny Crwys-Williams in November 2008: "I became more comfortable with her politically than with my mother." His mother died in 2005, but Malema has remained very close to his granny – he still phones her every day of his life.

Malema was only nine years old when he ran away from home and sneaked onto a bus carrying ANC members to

Johannesburg to see Nelson Mandela, who had just been released from jail after 27 years behind bars. When he returned home the next day, family members say, he was a different boy. In 1993 he ran away again, this time to attend the funeral of MK and SACP struggle icon Chris Hani, who had been assassinated by a right-wing fanatic.

Malema gets vague when asked about his earliest political activities, but stories abound of how he joined the ANC's Masupatsela (trailblazers) movement at the age of nine and how the local comrades taught him to make petrol bombs and barricades of burning tyres when he was only 12. ANC activists in Seshego confirm that Malema was a "child activist", trained ANC marshal and that he could toyi-toyi and sing liberation songs long before he went to high school.

He was only 14 when he became leader of the ANC Youth League in his home town. At 16 he was chairman of the Congress of South African Students (Cosas) in Limpopo and was elected its national president four years later.

How does one explain Malema's complete obsession with the ANC and politics in general since even before adolescence? He has repeatedly stated that he is not interested in getting married, because he is "married to the ANC"; he has only ever read political books, all biographies of ANC politicians; he says his "whole being belongs to the ANC"; he says even when he goes to clubs or restaurants to socialise he only talks about politics.

Perhaps growing up without a father – he says he has never known his father and has no need to get to know him – could explain a lot. When Crwys-Williams asked him whether not having a father left a gap in his life, he responded: "Perhaps those conditions made us to understand why there is a need for us to participate in the struggle and fight against the injustice caused by the apartheid regime. When you grow up under people who appreciate you and who are always there to support you, that gap, you don't feel it. Because in the ANC, the leaders of the ANC have played a father figure role in my life and they still do that even today."

Malema failed grade 8 and had to repeat grade 9, after, he says, he had been expelled for political activities. He only wrote his matric exams when he was 21. He wasn't a great student: in 2008 the media got hold of his matric results and revealed that he had just scraped through, failing both mathematics and woodwork. His school friends at Mohla-kaneng High maintain that this was more a consequence of his preoccupation with political activities than due to a lack of intelligence or an inability to learn. Observing him across his desk in Luthuli House it doesn't appear as if a lack of grey matter is one of his shortcomings.

But his weak academic background has probably contributed to his strong anti-intellectual streak. His full-frontal attack on the then Minister of Education, Naledi Pandor, for having a "fake American accent" (she has an English accent, actually) and several snide remarks about Thabo Mbeki's intellectualism, are examples. Malema is also fond of telling interviewers that many senior leaders are the products of "squatter camps and villages rather than universities", and that university degrees "don't guarantee wisdom". He told the *Sowetan* in an interview that he was very proud of Jacob Zuma "who was not educated at universities in London or America, but was taught by his own people in Nkandla".

(*Sunday Times* journalist and author Fred Khumalo once wrote about Malema, whom he called an ihlongandlebe or "contumelious nincompoop": "On second thoughts, I think I have to thank the gods of academia for denying Malema the stamina for rigorous study. Imagine a highly educated Malema.")

Malema's leadership of Cosas was marked by violent and unruly behaviour, especially during a march on the Gauteng Department of Education in Johannesburg in 2002 when Cosas members looted shops, vandalised property and stole from street traders. In 2003, when he was objecting to fraud and theft charges brought against Winnie Madikizela-Mandela, he declared that Cosas would burn down the jail if she were to be locked up.

Malema says he was a "fundamentalist" in his youth. He told Crwys-Williams: "When you grow up, you grow up a

"

fundamentalist, a communist hard-core, you think everything has got to do with communism." When asked whom
he wanted to meet most, he said: "You always have this
ambition that perhaps one day one should have a chance to
talk to Fidel (Castro) and hear where they come from with
this background. Because, you know that amongst the re-
maining communists Fidel represents the real communism."

Malema was elected president at the chaotic 2008
national conference of the Youth League at Mangaung in
Bloemfontein, where the delegates displayed the worst behaviour ever recorded at an ANC event. Mostly drunk, they
disrupted speakers and made sure no real discussion could
take place. The conference had to be dismissed eventually,
but not before the election of the top five leaders had taken
place and Malema came out victorious (it was alleged that
he spent vast amounts of money during his campaign). The
prevailing image of the conference will be the young dele-
gate, probably under the influence of alcohol, pulling down
his pants and flashing his bare bottom at opponents of Malema's candidature.

Another conference had to be scheduled at the Nasrec
conference centre outside Johannesburg months later to
elect the rest of the league's national executive committee,
an event that was the opposite of the Mangaung conference.
Quietly and with no big upsets, the conference drafted its

resolutions and elected the rest of the leadership. No one was surprised by the turnaround – this time the stakes were not as high. The supporters of Jacob Zuma knew that Malema would be a key factor in the 2009 election campaign, and they needed to make sure their man got the job. Once that had been sorted out at Mangaung, there was little to lose and the Nasrec conference went off without a glitch.

From Young Lion to Jelly Tsotsi[1]

The 2009 ANC election campaign saw Malema rise in the same populist manner in which his hero, Peter Mokaba, his mentor, Fikile Mbalula, and his party president, Jacob Zuma, had made their mark on South African society.

In his first public address as the new Youth League president, he urged his followers at a Youth Day rally to "take up arms and kill for Zuma" to ensure that he becomes the president of the country. This statement resulted in a summons from the Human Rights Commission, but was so powerful that it was almost immediately imitated by Cosatu general secretary Zwelinzima Vavi. The latter had to accompany him to a hearing ordered by the commission, which gave Malema a slap on the wrist, warning the young leader to refrain from such comments in future.

The ANC leadership did not rebuke Malema and Vavi for their threats of violence. Neither did they protest when Malema used dangerous language in referring to opposition parties in July 2008: "We must intensify the struggle to eliminate the remnants of counter-revolution, which include the DA and a loose coalition of those who want to use state power to block the ANC president's ascendancy

---

1 Jelly Tots + tsotsi: The name given to him by a *Sunday Times* columnist

14

to the highest office of the land." No wonder that shortly after the election the veterans of Umkhonto weSizwe, the military wing of the ANC during the struggle against apartheid, threatened to make the DA-ruled Western Cape "ungovernable" and the National Taxi Association threatened to "kill anyone who gets in our way" if their demands around a new Bus Rapid Transit public transport system weren't met.

Despite a roar of protest from the media and civil society, Malema emerged from this controversy more popular than ever before and secure in the knowledge that his statements, however outrageous, would carry the implicit approval of his party (the ANC refused to call Malema to order) and that he could show up Chapter Nine institutions like the Human Rights Commission as toothless and lacking in courage to take on real power. Malema now had reason to believe his views found resonance in his party. He demonstrated his peculiar knack for getting people's backs up – which he would use with great success during the election campaign.

The Youth League is a body that considers itself to be autonomous from the mother body and therefore planned its own 2009 campaign. In its quest for controversy and to establish itself as "the vanguard of the ANC", it decided to visit two places where no ANC group had ever dared to go: Nongoma in the heartland of the Inkatha Freedom Party in KwaZulu-Natal and the white mini-"volkstaat" of Orania.

These were the two highlights for Malema during the election campaign.

Says Malema in his seventh-floor corner office in Luthuli House: "It was nice to go and break new ground in Nongoma, when everyone was saying you can't go there. Some of the older Youth League leaders were saying, why do you want to cause the ANC heart attacks?"

Malema got into a slanging match with the IFP Youth Brigade (he called the IFP "a Mickey Mouse cultural organisation") and even IFP leader Mangosuthu Buthelezi was drawn into the threats and insults. "It is clear that Mr Malema, who is still at an age younger than the number of years I have served my country, does not understand the unspoken rules of politics," Buthelezi said. The fear that the conflict could erupt in bloodshed similar to that of the years before the 1994 election was raised by all sides.

But it was argued afterwards that Malema's Nongoma adventure had demystified the so-called IFP no-go areas and made it easier for locals to vote for the ANC, whereas they may have been too afraid before. The fact that KwaZulu-Natal was the only area in the country where the ANC didn't lose ground in the elections – it gained a massive 943 481 votes compared to 2004 – added to the credit Malema was given for his role in the election campaign. (Zuma's own ethnic identity, disaffection in the IFP and a well-run election campaign by the ANC are other reasons for the ANC's good results in the province.)

Orania was the other perceived no-go area. There was a sharp intake of breath nationally when Malema announced that he was going to visit the right-wing outpost.

"The ANC never had posters in Orania, we went to put posters there and engage with the Afrikaners' community," says Malema proudly. "For the first time in the history of Orania there were three votes for the ANC.

"Those 700 community members – they don't vote with blacks. I enjoyed my stay there in Orania; we left before five o'clock and we did everything. We drank tea from them in the same cup, there were no special cups [for us]. That one thing that is so sweet – koeksisters – we were also provided those. It is a privilege for a black person to be given such things there. You're a labourer, you have no relationship with that area. We had a very frank and open meeting there of what we think of each other and South Africa. Quite an experience. Since 1994 there were no other leaders who have visited those fundamentalists." (Nelson Mandela travelled to Orania to visit Hendrik Verwoerd's widow, Betsie, in 1994.)

He maintains his visit doesn't mean he condones the behaviour of the volkstaters. "We are working on them and their mentality; we need to be very patient. You don't need

"

to be harsh on that person, you need to put that person more closer, so that person comes to appreciate that you are not that monster that you are projected to be. And the more they stay very far from us, the more they will deny themselves an opportunity to learn and appreciate the culture of Africans, learning and appreciating Afrikaners, and Afrikaans as a language."

As in the case of the Nongoma visit, Malema says he did not consult with Jacob Zuma about the proposed visit. "We only carried out the message of the manifesto."

In Orania, Malema showed a side of himself that is seldom seen. Lizel Steenkamp of the Sunday newspaper *Rapport* wrote that she was watching Malema interact with the people of Orania through a window of the hall where they met: "The man inside looks like Julius, but he speaks a different language to the one we know him speaking. He is charming. He is composed (bedaard). But more importantly: he is more conciliatory than ever before. He asks: come back and teach us to live sustainably like you're doing at Orania. We don't want your money, he almost begs. It is your expertise without which South Africa is poorer."

It was after this visit to Orania that the idea of Malema as a "second Mandela" began gaining ground. It was first mentioned by Zwelinzima Vavi, but also by ANC NEC member (and, after the elections, Minister of Human Settlements) Tokyo Sexwale. (Malema said in an interview just before the 2009 elections that Sexwale was "one of my close comrades, one who doesn't speak in the papers but who engages me directly".)

Vavi told a gathering of the South African Commercial, Catering and Allied Workers' Union (Saccawu) in the Johannesburg City Hall: "[Mandela] came as a very militant leader of the Youth League. He turned tables around, he was absolutely as intolerant in a way to our leaders as Julius Malema is now. [Mandela] moved from being that difficult and militant to being an icon and one of the most admired leaders worldwide."

During the election campaign Malema and his colleagues in the Youth League made it their duty to attack DA leader Helen Zille at every possible opportunity. "Every time I speak she must be angry, that is my responsibility," he said on occasion. Labelling her black colleagues in the party as mere "garden boys who smile at the madam", Malema then took it to a more personal level, calling Zille a "fake" and "ugly", referring to Zille's admission to having had botox treatment to her face. After the DA won the Western Cape provincial election race convincingly, the insults became even more intense.

In a Youth League statement that was released while Malema was on study leave (he was doing a diploma in youth development), Zille's cabinet was referred to as consisting of her "boyfriends and concubines" because it was an all-male cabinet. She appointed them because she wanted to continue sleeping with them, the League said. On his return to his office, Malema announced that if he had been the one releasing the statement "it would have been even worse".

The secretary general of the ANC, Gwede Mantashe, said afterwards the Youth League's remarks had embarrassed the ANC. But Malema remains boisterous: "After that statement we attended a meeting of the ANC on the Monday and nobody raised any disappointment. Apart from reading in the papers and the statement, there has never been anything to say 'look, we don't agree with you on one two three' – those who released the statement should perhaps think twice about saying it and appreciate that the Youth League is helping them, because they couldn't degenerate to Zille's level. They are politicians, they are leaders, they must be diplomatic; we are not politicians or leadership, we are learning to be those.

"We are activists, and our work is to defend our leadership. So we had to go for her [Zille] in the manner which we did, to put her in her rightful place, and we succeeded."

But he started calling her "that racist little girl", although she is 30 years older than him. He also threatened to "flood" the Western Cape with black ANC-aligned youths from the Eastern Cape to oust the DA. The only time the ANC leadership really reprimanded Malema was when he had insulted one of their own.

This was after Malema had addressed hordes of protesters at the Tshwane University of Technology and had accused then Education Minister Naledi Pandor of not intervening in the workers' and students' grievances with management. "She must use her fake accent to address our problems," Malema told the crowd who later became violent, throwing stones at police officers. He said she spent too much time using her "American accent" and not enough on her work. (She actually has a British accent because she lived in England before 1994 and studied at the University of London.) The ANC forced Malema to apologise to Pandor in person and to release a letter of unconditional apology, stating: "I acknowledge that the remarks I made against you were uncalled for and might have disappointed and hurt you." Several months later, Malema does not look too sorry. "The minister intervened. We think we were very successful," he says.

The Youth League's arrogance towards leadership can be attributed to its undeniable media savvy. It knows how to be controversial and Malema is often in headlines and on newspaper posters, to the envy of other ANC leaders.

Malema's moral outrage at Zille's "sexism", which supposedly led her to appoint an all-male cabinet, stands exposed when compared to his remarks about women. The most notorious were about the woman who had accused Zuma of raping her, leading to his controversial trial for

❝

rape, of which he was acquitted. "When a woman didn't enjoy it, she leaves early in the morning. Those who had a nice time will wait until the sun comes out, request breakfast and ask for taxi money. In the morning, that lady requested breakfast and taxi money. You can't ask for money from somebody who raped you."

Malema claimed the ANC won the youth vote by making the ANC "cool". Part of that was projecting a lifestyle image that the youth would find aspirational.

He insists that he lives within his means, but his rise to riches happened in a flash – he's never had a job outside the ANC. Parties are held at the trendiest clubs in Johannesburg, where there is no limit to the consumption of Johnnie Walker Black Label whisky and Veuve Clicquot French champagne. He lives in a big, smart house in upmarket Sandton and is always seen in expensive cars, from BMWs to Lexuses to Mercedes Benzes.

Very comfortable in designer labels such as Fabiani, Malema insists that his flashy lifestyle shouldn't be an issue. "It's not me, it is this office. When I come here they give me a cellphone, a laptop, and they're trying to make my work easier. I don't know which car is which one. When they come to me and say, 'chief, we are using this car today', I get in and we go."

There is nothing wrong with a flashy lifestyle, he says, "if you can afford it". "We have deployed many young people in parliament, their salaries are far beyond the duties they are responsible for. They don't have kids, they don't have big families. So if they think they must invest their money in houses, cars, why stop them? They are doing that legally. As long as they don't forget where they come from and their obligation of serving the working class. The car that I drive means it meets my salary and the ANC car scheme. The house that I have, it means my salary can afford it, so I didn't rob anybody, I didn't take from the poor to have what I have."

Then Malema gets to the main rationale for his (and supposedly for other ANC personalities') ostentatious lifestyle: "If we are going to refuse the youth to drive these cars it means they are only good for white youth. Ours will never drive those cars. So we must sit and appreciate the good things by whites and not by one of our own. That's what we're trying to break."

In a similar vein he told the *Sowetan* in December 2008: "We are the elite that has been deliberately produced by the ANC as part of its policy to close the gap between whites and blacks in this country. It was the ANC that made it possible that, as part of the elite, some of us are now able to live in the suburbs."

Malema admits that patience is no virtue for him. He describes his leadership style as "down to earth" but impatient with change. He uses the words militant, radical and

"

revolutionary a lot in describing himself and his organisation. "We are radical, impatient with change; if you want to see things happening they must happen now. So that's what characterises who we are."

Malema may be tactically clever and politically street-smart when it comes to the disaffected youth, but he is definitely not one of the greatest political theoreticians in the ANC. For instance, he refuses to read newspapers. When Crwys-Williams asked him about this during her interview with him on Talk Radio 702, he said: "I've listened to people who read papers. They replace political education through editorial comments. I don't want to suffer from that illness. To hear politicians say Malema is a problem – to me that person has replaced the political language through editorial comment, because that is how they call it on the big post: Malema this, Malema that.

"Now I don't want to be influenced by newspapers. I live amongst the people. I'm on the ground . . . I don't need newspapers to replace the honest view of the ordinary masses, because I've got access to those people."

When asked how his world view was informed if he didn't read newspapers, he said: "When I want to know about a certain country I will make a research about it and go through the relevant material. I don't just read everything that is going to mislead me."

But Malema probably also has reason for being cynical

about newspapers' treatment of him. Reporters have milked every statement he's made for something controversial and have prodded him to come up with yet another outrageous utterance.

He tells the story of how he once challenged Tokyo Sexwale to write him a speech which he would then read in public. "I said to him by the time you read it in the newspaper, Comrade Tokyo, you will think it isn't your speech, because they will find a creative way to twist it and make it look horrible. And you'll be afraid to be associated with that speech by the time they're printing it."

"

. . . .

Running dog or hero of the revolution?

Malema evokes strong reactions from those outside the ANC and his youthful fan base. Former ANC MP and parliamentary whip David Dalling voiced the opinion of many when he said, "Malema is an uneducated, loud-mouthed, ignorant and arrogant lout, and an embarrassment to both the ANC and all of South Africa. As Anne Robinson would say, 'You are the weakest link. Goodbye.' President Zuma should tell him to go." A senior former cabinet minister says with considerable venom in his voice: "Malema is nothing but a running dog. It is scandalous that Zuma and Mantashe are tolerating his despicable behaviour – or shall I say encouraging it." A former youth activist, Siyanda Mhlongo, wrote in the *Sowetan* that Malema's utterances were "primitive, barbaric, backward".

Cope leader Terror Lekota called Malema a "child soldier", typical of those who have caused so much destruction in Africa. He said Malema's political intolerance and threats of violence showed the ANC's descent into iron-fisted authoritarianism. "Malema says, 'If you do not do what we say, then we will take up arms and kill you.' And you still want us to think of Malema as a joke?"

But a University of Cape Town student, Motheo Moleko, gave a different, fascinating insight in a piece he wrote for news24.com after Malema had addressed a meeting on the campus just before the April elections. Malema "cemented his position as the politician least afraid to provoke and most likely to grossly polarise his detractors from his supporters," Moleko wrote. "Yet, amidst the cheers, boos and theatrics, I believe I witnessed something far more interesting – the imminence of a new political celebrity. On his rare visit to UCT, I was less surprised with what he had to say than I was surprised at the effect he had on people."

Moleko wrote that Malema drew about 700 students without much pre-publicity. Apart from a few DA hecklers, the crowd mostly loved him. Malema inspired them, he wrote; "I witnessed many of those sitting on the fence becoming believers of the 'glorious revolution' Julius spoke of." Malema was "not everybody's cup of tea", Moleko continued, "but there is a lot more going on under the hood than some have been led to believe. Furthermore, whether those who witnessed him liked what they saw or found it intolerable, every person who walked out of the Beattie Lecture Theatre onto University Avenue was emotionally charged and was wanting more."

In Luthuli House itself, those who do not love or hero-worship Malema fear him – or tolerate him because he serves their purposes. Most make sure that they stay on his right side.

About three million new voters registered for the April 2009 elections. Most of those must have been young and black. Malema and his lieutenants like to remind the ANC leadership that the Youth League delivered most of these votes to the ANC. That made sure that the ANC ended up with 65,9% of the total vote, despite the breakaway by Cope and the growth of the DA.

It seems fairly safe to assume that Malema's value to the mainstream ANC is the fact that the disaffected black youth, angry and resentful that their prospects have not dramatically improved in recent years, are attracted by Malema's rudeness, militancy and blanket defiance. His power gives them a little, by proxy.

Opposition parties claim Malema is being shamelessly used as a tool by the senior leadership of the ANC to "do their dirty work for them". The ANC denies this, naturally, and reminds people that the ANC Youth League can legitimately claim some autonomy. Some leaders privately tell reporters that they don't take Malema seriously and that's why they find it unnecessary to constantly repudiate and discipline him. But there is sufficient reason to believe that Zuma himself and several of his senior comrades in the ANC's national executive have consciously exploited Malema's blustering style and scare tactics to their own advantage.

One of those leaders reluctantly conceded as much: "All those who claimed to have left the ANC because of Julius's antics would have left the ANC anyway. When the IFP's

Koos van der Merwe said before the elections that Malema was the opposition parties' best weapon, he didn't know what he was talking about. Sure, he embarrasses us occasionally, but it does no lasting damage; we simply say he's young and still has to learn. On the other hand, he's brought real value to the party at election time and his role in getting Zuma where he is now, instead of in jail, should not be underestimated."

Whatever his political future, Julius Malema has made sure of his place in the history books in the important new era in South African politics after the Polokwane revolution of December 2007.

Max du Preez and Mandy Rossouw

....

Malema on Malema

"I'm an ordinary young person
who's grown up here in South Africa,
from a township, who has no intention –
none whatsoever – to scare people."

NOVEMBER 2008

In an interview with Jenny Crwys-Williams on Talk Radio 702.

"

On loyalty to Zuma

"We are prepared to die for Zuma . . . We are prepared to take up arms and kill for Zuma."

JUNE 2008

Malema's promise at a Youth Day rally in Thaba Nchu in the Free State.

On "killing for Zuma" – an apology

"If we did sound like we're inciting violence,
we are very sorry. That was not our intention;
we'll never incite violence. We will never do anything
unconstitutional. We are law-abiding citizens of this
country and we will protect the Constitution
of this republic. We fought for it and we stand by it."

NOVEMBER 2008

On the "killing for Zuma" furore

"It's not that we are saying the same thing
but this is an electrified [sic] election.
We've got it coming from all corners. It's highly
charged. The only thing we have to be sure about
is that we do not upset the electorate."

NOVEMBER 2008

On Naledi Pandor

"We've got a minister who's spending too much
time using an American accent without
assisting our people. That is the main problem.
Let the minister use that fake accent to address
our problems and not to behave like a spoilt minister."

FEBRUARY 2009

*Malema intervened in a dispute between management and students
at the Tshwane University of Technology over student fees and
threatened then Minister of Education, Naledi Pandor, to sort it out or else . . .
It was the only comment which the ANC condemned in the
strongest terms and for which they forced Malema to apologise.*

"

On Naledi Pandor, again

"If there is a failure to listen,
she knows what will happen to her."

FEBRUARY 2009

To Naledi Pandor – an apology

"I acknowledge that the remarks I made against you
were uncalled for and might have disappointed
and hurt you . . . We assert our most sincere
and unconditional apology to you and the
ANC for what we accept to have been
uncalled-for remarks."

FEBRUARY 2009

"

On being reprimanded by the ANC

"I have never seen a parent pack his bags and leave his home because his child is rude. To do so is to abdicate your duties. You should whip the child into line. Those who say we are disrespectful say so because they want us to worship them."

MARCH 2009

On Zuma's education

"Zuma was taught by people on the ground.
He is the most educated president. Economics is simple –
put bread on the table."

JANUARY 2009

"

On Zuma's rape accuser

"When a woman didn't enjoy it,
she leaves early in the morning. Those who had
a nice time will wait until the sun comes out,
request breakfast and ask for taxi money.
In the morning, that lady requested breakfast
and taxi money. You can't ask for money
from somebody who raped you."

JANUARY 2009

*ANC president and later South African president Zuma went
on trial for rape in December 2005, and was acquitted in May 2006
on all charges. Malema was addressing students at the
Cape Peninsula University of Technology's Bellville campus.*

On Zuma's rape trial

"Zuma was accused of raping a woman,
although he did not rape the woman, uphiwe nje
[he was just given the sexual favour], he got fired."

JANUARY 2009

"

On Zuma going to prison

"If you arrest him, he will lead us from prison.
We are not afraid to be led
by a president in orange clothes."

JULY 2008

*Zuma was facing charges of fraud which, if convicted,
would have seen him serve a jail term. Orange
refers to the colour of the clothes prisoners wear.*

On Zuma's corruption charges

"But what is wrong with the president of the country being in and out of court?"

JANUARY 2009

"

On Zuma's relationship with Schabir Shaik

"How many of you have helped wash a
comrade's car or pay their children's school fees?
That's how the ANC taught us. It then means we are
all corrupt, because that's how we live."

JANUARY 2009

*Judge Hilary Squires found the relationship between Zuma and his
financial adviser Schabir Shaik, who went to jail in 2005 for corruption,
to be one of "mutually beneficial symbiosis".*

On criminal activities of ANC members

"It can never be acceptable that members of the ANC
and the Youth League get involved in criminal
activities whether through theft of public monies
intended for the poor or stabbing fellow
comrades because they believe they are entitled to
ANC membership. These are the rotten apples
that must be uprooted from our midst without mercy."

JULY 2008

Malema's warning against corruption in the ANC.

On Zuma's corruption charges

"Leave Zuma to the voters to punish him.
If he is so corrupt and he must be punished,
let the voters do that."

FEBRUARY 2009

*Malema was explaining that the people, not the judicial process,
should have the final say on Zuma's corruption charges.*

On corruption

"You must never role model a rich person
who can't explain how they got rich. In the ANC
we must not have corrupt people as role models.
Corrupt means a simple thing – you can't explain
the big amount in your bank account.
In less than a year you have got everything.
Yesterday you were down and out,
but today you have everything, which
shows in your fancy dress code."

MARCH 2009

*Malema was telling a crowd in Pretoria to be suspicious of
corruption when people get rich quickly.*

On changing the Constitution

"We are not going to agree to any changing of the Constitution to accommodate an individual. This is the Constitution of the people of South Africa, and it would never be amended to suit an individual . . . We are convinced that by the time we go to the inauguration, our president would have been cleared of these allegations."

JANUARY 2009

After the Constitutional Court had reinstated corruption charges against Jacob Zuma in 2007, there was much talk of changing the Constitution to exempt a sitting president from prosecution.

On "dark forces" acting against the ANC

"Judges can be spoken to by any other person,
knowing the tendency of these ones who are against us.
They, the 'dark forces', travel at night. They've got
the potential to do anything . . ."

JANUARY 2009

*After Pietermaritzburg High Court Judge Chris Nicholson's judgement
that corruption charges against Zuma were unlawful
was overturned by the Supreme Court of Appeal in Bloemfontein.*

On the Sonke Gender Justice Advocacy Group

"The black faces you see in front – those are not
real faces, they represent the whites who are
opposed to African leadership. The imperialists
and the whites who are still representing
the past are using this organisation."

JULY 2009

*Malema's response to the Sonke Gender Justice Advocacy Group,
who took Malema to the Equality Court
after his statement on rape in January 2009.*

On Sonke, again

"We will never apologise to some Mickey Mouses
who want to put pressure on us."

JULY 2009

Malema's response outside the Equality Court after the
matter was postponed to August 2009.

On dropping the corruption charges against Zuma

"We don't want to speculate, we will wait
for an announcement. But if that is their thinking
[to drop the charges], then they [NPA] must have
courage and not be intimidated by these
noise-makers. That would be good as it would
be in the interests of South Africa."

APRIL 2009

On forgiveness

"Bulelani Ngcuka, McCarthy, whatever else they did,
we should say, as a South African society,
let's close this chapter, let's move forward."

APRIL 2009

*Former chief prosecutor Bulelani Ngcuka achieved fame for
declaring that there was a prima facie case against Zuma,
but that the NPA (National Prosecuting Authority) would not
prosecute. Former Scorpions' head Leonard McCarthy was accused
of working with Ngcuka against Zuma.*

"

On Zuma, again

"For those of you saying Zuma should not
be president, [you] are daydreaming . . . He will be
the best-ever first president of the Republic."

APRIL 2009

On commissions of enquiry

"Let's go back to 1994 . . . those who are saying, 'let's arrest', are not putting the interests of the country first . . . If you support commissions, if you support charges, you are effectively saying even when Zuma is not charged, he must go and give evidence against the people because they are charged in relation to him. So again, our president, having not been charged, will still have to go to court to give evidence and that is something we don't want."

APRIL 2009

The government has been under pressure to have a commission of enquiry into the multi-billion rand arms acquisition deal approved in 1999, which has led to a stream of allegations of corruption and fraud.

"
. . . .

On Zuma's return to the Union Buildings

"On 9 May Zuma will be in Pretoria,
where they expelled [him] like a dog, as the
most important revolutionary."

APRIL 2009

On Jacob Zuma as president

"He's not Mr Know-It-All,
he accepts criticism."

MAY 2009

"

On the future of Jacob Zuma

"We are not supporters of Zuma, who is an individual,
but of the ANC. Before Polokwane the ANC was
in the pocket of one individual. It was a one-man show.
Zuma would be the one to follow if he does not
follow the programme of the ANC. If he deviates,
he will definitely be redeployed."

APRIL 2009

*Shortly before the elections Malema insinuated to a crowd
in Port Elizabeth that Zuma could have the same fate as Mbeki.*

On politicians who can be replaced

"Whether you are a premier, an MEC or a mayor, nobody is stopping you from leaving. You might make newspaper headlines today with your resignation, but tomorrow you're forgotten when [Barack] Obama and Zuma once again dominate the headlines."

NOVEMBER 2008

On politicians who can be replaced, again

"Politicians are the easiest to replace . . . we will
move forward and they will carry on with the
programmes which are there."

NOVEMBER 2008

On changing leaders

"If you resign, Terror Mosiuoa Lekota,
then General Siphiwe Nyanda will take over as
defence minister. You don't advertise, you don't call
for interviews, it's not a long process."

SEPTEMBER 2008

After former president Thabo Mbeki had been fired,
Malema made the point that there is no scarcity of leaders
in the ANC and therefore no need to lament Mbeki's departure.
To change leaders is an easy, straightforward process.

"

On a two-thirds majority
"We are tired of a two-thirds majority. Our aim
is a 'three-thirds' majority."

APRIL 2009

On opinion polls

"That Markinor is a group of some people who
have some agenda which will be defeated on April 22."

FEBRUARY 2009

*After a Markinor survey had found only 16% of South Africans have
confidence in him. April 22 was the date of the 2009 elections.*

On the Western Cape

"No research has shown that the ANC will be
out of power. If it gets less than two thirds,
it will still be in power. Even if in the Western Cape
we lose, it will be through a coalition of crooks."

APRIL 2009

On the opposition

"Don't provoke us, it is us [the ANC] who brought
the nonsensical apartheid regime down.
No opposition [party] will ever defeat the ANC.
We want them all to combine so we can defeat them."

APRIL 2009

At a rally in Cape Town to cheers from Malema's supporters.

"

On campaigning in hospitals

"But he said he was worried that the DA
would also want to do the same thing,
so we said we are not going to campaign.
We were merely wishing people well."

APRIL 2009

*The superintendent of Dora Nginza Hospital in Port Elizabeth
kicked Malema and his sidekicks out when he found them
campaigning on the hospital's grounds.*

On Orania

"We thought well-armed Afrikaners
would stop the blacks."

MARCH 2009

*Malema visited the Afrikaner "volkstaat" during
the April 2009 election campaign.*

On being a decoy

"I was the decoy. While Helen Zille was calling me names, Jacob Zuma was sprinting to the Union Buildings."

APRIL 2009

Malema claimed his utterances made during an address to students in East London three days before the 2009 elections had been part of their election strategy.

On Nando's – Malema's first response

"I have no problem with the advertisement because Nando's is trying to be creative. But if they use me they must pay."

APRIL 2009

Fast-food chain Nando's created a puppet called Julius in an advertising campaign, evoking much response from the public.

On Nando's – his second response

"We don't have money to advertise on
TV and radio, but we have strength to close down
every Nando's outlet."

APRIL 2009

Nando's advertising campaign was withdrawn 24 hours after they had
met with the ANC Youth League, who threatened militant action.

On Nando's – for the last time

"I don't know what's happening with Nando's.
We are running this country and we
cannot be concerned about chickens."

APRIL 2009

On going to parliament

"Not any time soon. I think parliament is for old people, don't you agree? It's not my favourite place."

JANUARY 2009

Malema had been nominated to be an ANC parliamentarian,
but he declined the offer.

On birthdays

"I don't celebrate my birthday. I'm a poor fellow,
and I can't afford to throw big parties."

JANUARY 2009

*Malema tried to highlight his "poverty" by claiming he would
have no lavish birthday celebrations. Which, incidentally, he did.*

"

On drinking

"I went to consult the doctor the next day because I was exhausted. There is no way I can miss a political engagement because I was drinking. Those who know me know that even if I slept at 5am, I would be up at 8am ready to work."

MARCH 2009

After Malema had missed a political engagement, he said his Youth League colleagues had organised a surprise birthday party for him, but that he had not stayed too long at the party as he was not feeling well.

On the ANC Youth League

"So far nobody has ever raised any issue, none whatsoever, with us on any utterance, on any position we have ever taken. We're breaking new ground on any topic, bringing life into any debate that you can think of. We sometimes even say things that old people are afraid to say."

NOVEMBER 2008

Malema was explaining why the ANC never reprimanded him for his comments.

"

On the Youth League conference in Mangaung

"Thugs and hooligans who believe they
can hold the organisation to ransom through
their despicable behaviour will be dealt with
in the harshest possible manner."

APRIL 2008

On being militant

"Nelson Mandela and Peter Mokaba
[the late ANC Youth League leader] did not
teach us to be afraid of anybody."

MARCH 2009

"

. . . .

On possible disruption at rallies

"This is no SABC election debate. This is the meeting of the ANC Youth League. If you disagree with us, go and convene your own meeting. We will deal with you ourselves. I will sort you both politically and physically."

APRIL 2009

After an election debate at the SABC had turned violent
when opposition party members became rowdy.

On the ANC Youth League, again

"The ANC Youth League is a political preparatory school for ANC leaders of tomorrow, a task it has executed diligently without fail throughout its existence."

JULY 2008

"

On the ANC Youth League, again

"We are in a political laboratory; never blame us if
we make mistakes, we are [just] learning."

APRIL 2009

On leadership in the ANC

"You don't need qualifications to lead in the ANC."

FEBRUARY 2009

On new deployees in government

"They must prove that they are not in government to enrich themselves."

APRIL 2009

Malema took issue with those whom the ANC put in government positions, reminding them not to fall prey to corruption.

On challenging authority

"We are not here to romanticise management, to play *The Bold and the Beautiful* with them. We are not here to play and they need to listen."

MARCH 2009

Malema promised that the university management issues at the Tshwane University of Technology would be dealt with promptly and would not continue in the fashion of soap operas.

"

On strikes

"We are going to be engaging Cosatu on the
possible strikes that are being planned all over.
We know many workers have demanded an increase –
in the past every time they demanded a certain
percentage, they ended up getting something close
to that. But the reality is that it may be different
this year and the workers will have to understand
the economic conditions that we find ourselves in.
We don't think engaging in lots of strikes is
going to help us come out of this situation."

MAY 2009

*Malema taking an unusual stance against workers,
urging them to rethink strike action.*

On a South African Airways strike

"From here, I will give the minister a
simple phone call to say 'We want you to intervene'
and that will happen, because she is a
minister of the ANC and we are the ANC."

FEBRUARY 2009

*After former Minister of Public Enterprises Brigitte Mabandla's failure
to deal more promptly with the SAA strike.*

On the University of Cape Town

"Forces that are opposed to our revolution are still here. We must change the management of this university and also the lecturers. This is our university, we must change the look of this university, it should reflect South Africa."

APRIL 2008

On claims of plotting

"The leadership of the ANC Youth League and the
YCL [Young Communist League] has other important
things to do, including campaigning for an
overwhelming ANC victory, than to discuss a plot
to unseat Prof Pityana . . . It is disgusting that a person
who regards himself as an intellectual would,
as a sign of desperation, receive and present lies as
truth to the public on broad daylight [sic]. Pityana
should stop wandering in the fast lane of paranoia and
begin answering his case."

MARCH 2009

*After Unisa's vice-chancellor, Barney Pityana, had accused
Malema of plotting against him to have him removed from his post.*

On Thabo Mbeki pushing people

"When you push Winnie Mandela on stage,
on Youth Day, you must know people see the ANC as
pushing old women around. Don't complain about
respect from young people, when you pushed
an icon on the stage of a youth event."

JANUARY 2009

*Former president Thabo Mbeki accidentally pushed
Winnie Madikizela-Mandela while they were on stage at a
Youth Day event in 2001.*

On charging Mbeki

"If you charge Mbeki you are inviting unnecessary sympathy for him because the highest price Mbeki paid was when we recalled him as president."

APRIL 2009

Suggestions were made by Zuma supporters that former president Thabo Mbeki should be charged after all corruption charges had been dropped against Zuma, citing political interference in the operations of the National Prosecuting Authority.

"

On Mbeki and the Congress of the People

"He is a Dalai Lama of Cope, he is a spiritual leader of Cope and he must come out in the open and declare he is ANC and not Cope."

MARCH 2009

Mbeki refused to campaign for the ANC after he had been axed as national president. Strong rumours insisted that he was the mastermind behind the ANC's breakaway group that later formed Cope.

On Mbeki, again

"We are closing a chapter of eight years of suffering under dictatorship."

On 22 April 2009, when South Africa went to the polls to elect its third post-1994 president.

On Mbeki at Jacob Zuma's inauguration

"There are conspirators among us who have
come to enjoy this day with fake smiles. We don't care
about them. We know who they are and we have closed
that chapter. They must accept defeat and that is why
they have come to witness what they have
thought was not possible."

MAY 2009

*Mbeki was invited by Zuma to see the latter being sworn in as
president and Malema claimed his smiles at the event were not genuine
because technically Zuma had unseated him.*

On Cope's sponsors

"They have left the ANC. Those are the forces who are working on us. Those that have left this organisation. They were doing it from within. They failed. Then they left. They're doing it from outside now because they think they can mobilise our people against this glorious movement and they are working with the imperialists, the former colonisers, to try and destabilise this country. It's an agenda to destabilise liberation movements in Africa."

JANUARY 2009

Cope was formed in December 2008 by disaffected ANC heavyweights broadly from the camp of recalled former president Thabo Mbeki.

"

On ANC leaders leaving for Cope

"They are a group of chancers who have
failed in the ANC. Just because they have not been
elected as leaders, they are [disappointed]."

NOVEMBER 2008

On members of Cope

"Their moves are well calculated . . . They are
well resourced. Don't under-estimate a man who is
well resourced in a capitalist society."

JANUARY 2009

On Cope leaders

"We were drinking with you on the corner, Cope, but now you walk tall. You claim to be men of the suburbs, but you are products of the squatter camps."

MARCH 2009

Cope spawned from the ANC and were ridiculed by their former comrades who knew the new Cope leaders' roots.

On Cope leaders and the arms deal

"Many of them did not benefit genuinely. They looted the ANC money. They stole money, they stole every big deal in South Africa including the arms deal, they stole that. They stole everything. They must leave our president on arms deal [sic]; he was in KwaZulu-Natal when they were stealing arms deal [sic], he was not national."

MARCH 2009

“

On Mvume Dandala

"Cope was formed because many of its founding
members said they could not be led by 'immoral'
leaders, but then did not find moral leaders
within their own ranks."

FEBRUARY 2009

Cope's presidential candidate, the former Methodist Church head and
bishop Mvume Dandala, was the party's answer to the perceived
dearth of moral leaders in the ANC.

On the black middle class

"The black middle class say we don't care about them, but we [the ANC] produced them, we opened the gates to the suburbs. They can't vote against the ANC – affirmative action and black economic empowerment are ANC policies."

MARCH 2009

This comment came after Cope had said it would win the votes of the black middle class.

"

On Terror Lekota

"That party will not take votes from the ANC
but will take votes from other opposition parties . . .
they are blue-light revolutionaries who can't imagine
their life without bodyguards and had forgotten how to
drive. Lekota is a factory fault who behaved like he
has never been to the ANC's political school."

OCTOBER 2008

Mosiuoa (Terror) Lekota was a co-founder of Cope.

On a councillor who jumped to Cope

"Let me tell them, they are also a disappointment
to their wives and children. Those councillors who
have resigned are inviting poverty into their homes.
Who is going to pay your salaries?
Remember as well, it doesn't mean that if you were a
councillor you were the best. The community might
not have wanted you, but just because you carried the
flag of the ANC, you were in that position."

NOVEMBER 2008

"

On Helen Zille

"When we say Zille represents . . . the apartheid system, we mean this. When they can't defeat them they must arrest them and lock them up."

FEBRUARY 2009

On Cope's Sam Shilowa

"He is an irresponsible father and a security guard."

NOVEMBER 2008

Cope's first deputy president, Mbhazima Shilowa,
the former premier of Gauteng, had defaulted on child support payments.

"

On Joe Seremane

"His role is to smile at the madam every time."

FEBRUARY 2009

*Seremane is the most senior black leader in the DA
and constantly ridiculed by the ANC.*

On Zille, again

"She is a colonialist and an imperialist and
uses Michael Jackson tactics."

FEBRUARY 2009

*Malema implied that Zille suffers, like the late Michael Jackson,
from too much cosmetic surgery.*

"

On Cope, again

"They are working with the imperialists; they are no different from the MDC [Zimbabwe's Movement for Democratic Change] and Kenyan Prime Minister Raila Odinga's party; they are puppets of the West."

JANUARY 2009

Malema accused Cope of being funded by Western countries –
an insult Robert Mugabe popularised.

On Zille, again

"She is plastic and not original, and
cannot stand a political hit."

MARCH 2009

"

On the DA Youth

"There is no DA Youth. The last time we had a
DA Youth was when they defected to the ANC.
There is no DA Youth in South Africa."

FEBRUARY 2009

On debating with the DA Youth

"I only debate with serious political youth formations.
Not a group of the racist Helen Zille's garden boys."

FEBRUARY 2009

DA youth leaders challenged Malema to a public debate,
a challenge he refused to take up.

"

"

On debating with the DA

"The reason why he, Ramulifho, wants a debate with Julius is because he wants promotion. He wants his name to be known that he took Julius on and I don't have time to be promoting small parties. They must get their own promotion. I think I should debate with Helen Zille because I don't think that man has that standard of political engagement."

MARCH 2009

During a conversation with Redi Direko on Talk Radio 702 after DA Youth leader Khume Ramulifho had challenged him to a pre-election debate.

On Helen Zille, again

"I do not understand why that racist Helen Zille tells people about our secrets because if she says I am an inkwenkwe then surely she cannot talk about something she has not seen before. She must stop being racist and dividing our people in Cape Town."

MARCH 2009

*DA leader Helen Zille called Malema an
uncircumcised boy after he had called her a "little racist girl".*

On Bantu Holomisa

"We recruited him into the ANC, but he could not
subject himself to the collective discipline of the ANC.
We showed him the door and he formed the UDM –
a one-man show."

MARCH 2009

*Malema was explaining that the ANC breakaway party, Cope,
would become an insignificant player on the political scene,
like Holomisa's United Democratic Movement (UDM). Holomisa,
who had come to power in a coup in the Transkei homeland,
was elected to the ANC's NEC as one of its most popular members
in 1994, but was expelled in 1996. He then formed the UDM.*

On Zille, again

"She is fake – even she had to go and do plastic surgery, she is not original. If you can fake your own face, what about the policies? It means you are a fake. If you look at the original picture, Helen Zille is very ugly. She really looks like a real apartheid agent."

APRIL 2009

On Mangosuthu Buthelezi

"We vow to recruit all his children and his wife, then recruit him [Mangosuthu] so that we can save him from himself. He's a dictator."

FEBRUARY 2009

Malema defied threats by the IFP leader to desist from campaigning in Nongoma, which is considered to be an IFP stronghold.

On Buthelezi, again

"He is undermining the intelligence of Zulus,
who do not vote on the basis of ethnicity; they vote
on the basis of policies."

MARCH 2009

“

On Helen Zille as premier

"We will never make up with Helen Zille – she is an enemy of the revolution . . . she's a racist and will remain a racist. She has a racist agenda of making the Western Cape a province for whites only. If she had a way as premier to declare [which] people she wants in the province . . . for sure by now she would have declared the Western Cape for whites only."

MAY 2009

On the by-elections in the Western Cape

"We did not lose the by-elections in the Western Cape. It was the judge who voted on behalf of the people of the Western Cape against the ANC. That was an undemocratic process, they [the other parties] shouldn't think that with the outcome of the Western Cape they've defeated the ANC."

DECEMBER 2008

The ANC failed to register for the by-elections of twelve candidates in time for the deadline in December 2008 and they were subsequently disqualified.

"

On Zille and migration

"As the Youth League we are going to encourage
many young people, especially those staying in the
Eastern Cape, to start applying for houses and sites in the
Western Cape, so that we have more blacks and Africans
going to Western Cape . . . to disappoint [Zille]."

MAY 2009

On Zimbabwe's land redistribution

"We agree with Mugabe on land redistribution,
but we think it should not be done at the expense of
the suffering of the people."

JANUARY 2009

"

On Robert Mugabe

"He must step down – we need a new president in Zim.
The Zanu-PF is not the problem, the problem is the
old man who is refusing to leave power.
So that's simple. And I don't know why the youth
of that country are not taking him on. Because it is their
own future, they must defend it now."

NOVEMBER 2008

*Malema decided to weigh in on the Zimbabwe issue, which many
in the ANC felt had not been properly handled by Mbeki.*

On the failure of capitalism

"At the moment, when the imperialist forces are accepting the failures of capitalism, we should ask whether the time has not arrived for the government to make sure the state owns the mines and other means of production as called for in the Freedom Charter."

JULY 2009

Malema was calling for nationalisation of the mines at the launch of the Youth League's political school.

On the media

"We must not be hoodwinked into believing lies and half-truths the prophets of doom are spreading about our revolutionary movement, the ANC. Those who stand on dark corners and proclaim that the ANC has lost its moral compass and has abandoned the Freedom Charter are merely spreading lies to advance their narrow, self-serving political agendas."

OCTOBER 2008

On the media, again

"Perhaps it is time we took the task upon ourselves
to educate the political imbeciles who believe
that because they have unfettered access to the media
they are opinion-makers. They deliberately rubbish
and distort the National Democratic Revolution
and what the ANC stands for in order to
achieve their narrow political ends."

OCTOBER 2008

"

On the ANC's vision

"Ours is a grand vision that aims to achieve a society where poverty is eradicated, our people live in peace side by side, free from any form of discrimination and all are equal before the law."

OCTOBER 2008

Malema said at a Youth League rally that the ANC would never be defeated, despite the criticism against the party.

On today's youth

"So we must speak out and never allow [ourselves] to be silenced because we are not ghosts. We must make our mark just like the youth of 1976 made theirs."

MARCH 2009

Former newspaper editor and television personality MAX DU PREEZ works as a political analyst, newspaper columnist and documentary film maker. He is the author of *Of Warriors, Lovers and Prophets – Unusual Stories from South Africa's Past* and its sequel, *Of Tricksters, Tyrants and Turncoats*. His other books include *Pale Native* and *Oranje Blanje Blues*. He received the coveted Nat Nakasa Award for courageous journalism from the SA National Editors' Forum in 2008 and was named the Yale Globalist International Journalist in 2006.

MANDY ROSSOUW is a senior political journalist for the *Mail & Guardian* newspaper where she specialises in international, African and domestic politics. She cut her teeth at the Johannesburg-based Afrikaans daily, *Beeld*, where she started her career as a political and parliamentary reporter. This is where the political bug bit her. She became the foreign correspondent in London for the Media24 group in 2006 and joined the *Mail & Guardian* in September 2007.